FROM BABBLE TO READING
CARRIE PEOPLES' READING SYSTEM

by

CARRIE PEOPLES

co-authored by

DANIELLE YETTE

Olympus Story House

FROM BABBLE TO READING

CARRIE PEOPLES' READING SYSTEM

INTRODUCTION

INFORMATION IS THE MOST VALUABLE COMMODITY ON EARTH. WE BUY AND SELL MORE INFORMATION THAN ANYTHING.

Children learn most of what they need in life between birth and five years old. They build learning processes and knowledge on that foundation with reiteration through our education processes. In order to ensure children have the base necessary it is imperative they receive the fundamental tools to process information prior to reaching school age.

Taking time to teach your children, first, personalizes the learning process. This shared experience will give you and your youngster the opportunity to bond through learning this foundation of our communication and educational processes. As you implement this reading system you, your child and your family will develop new areas of independence as well as dependence for the purpose of knowledge building. Families interacting within this realm is a warm and beautiful experience for all. Confidence toward learning will develop and grow naturally. Success comes with a child's understanding and acceptance that strengthening human nature and purpose in life is constant. We must consciously and continuously build positive KNOWLEDGE, SKILLS, ABILITIES AND ATTITUDES to compete in our rapidly changing society.

Think, corporations invest millions of dollars on retraining adult workers to learn communication skills: listening, writing, reading, and data usage. By developing these skills early, you are ensuring that children are ready with essential skills to be at the forefront for opportunities awaiting them in their futures.

1. Work with each child for about twenty to thirty minutes every day.

In order for each child to gain the understanding of the importance of learning to read, it must be proven by the amount of time given by the adults in their lives. By implementing this process on a daily basis it will become an enjoyable habit that is looked forward to. It is a chance to spend quality time with each child, while encouraging and enabling verbal and mental growth.

2. Ask each child to tell you a story.

Children have a wealth of words and ideas they want to get out of their brains, however, at times they do not have the abilities necessary to verbalize their thoughts. This process gives each child the chance to tell you anything from what they had for dinner the night before to the fantastic journeys they go on with their imaginary friends. This is a free space for each child. It is not a time for them to be corrected or guided.

Some children will have more fun and feel less stressed by creating story boxes to build a story first, before the writing exercise. This can be done with miniature items made by hand or purchased anywhere (tiny characters, buildings, vehicles, food, animals, grass, furniture, sand, cars, balloons...). Children enjoy creating scenes from their imagination with items before writing about them.

3. You will record them as they speak.

You will need a device to record the story each child tells you. This can be recorded using numerous devices: the child's iPad, Chromebook, a cell phone, or any other device that will reach the end result of recording.

Explain to each child what it means to be recorded and show them how the recording process works so they are comfortable. Allow them to speak into the instrument you have chosen and play it back so they can hear themselves and have a firm understanding of the operations being used. Make sure to have each child speak loudly enough for the recordings to catch each word. This will also assist you with writing down each story, in case any words are missed, depending on the speed (excitement) of each child.

4. You will write down what they say exactly as they say it with no corrections.

Write down each word exactly as the child says it. Make no corrections. Let the story be owned completely by the child. The words are their own. This will be an exact depiction of each child's thoughts. It will assist the child in understanding their words and thoughts in the future. It will also lead to an accurate depiction of where they began the reading process.

5. One page per day

The story from each child should amount to one page per day. That is all that is needed for this process. The number of words from each child and day may vary. This process should be enjoyable.

6. Each day, have your child read the story told the previous day.

To begin each portion of time spent together for reading, have the child read the story they told the previous day. It may not be exact, or what is written on the page at all. This will get more precise as time goes on. Each child will gain a deeper understanding as they become more aware of the process.

7. At the end of each week, have the child read the five stories told to you.

At the end of each week, have your child dictate each story told to you. They may still add or exclude information and that is alright. Your child is beginning an editing process to allow recognition of accuracies and errors. By having produced and read their own stories throughout the week they will easily take ownership and recall details. Give praises for a job well done!

8. When you get about twenty to thirty stories, begin to make their "books" with cardboard and nice material or paper as a cover. Soon they will have many "books".

Have the materials necessary for the creation of your child's "books": nice paper with lines, cardboard, material (cloth or durable, designed paper), glue or paste, pencils or markers.

By keeping the stories in order by date you will be able to monitor the progression of your child. Creating the "books" is a way for each child to nurture their stories and feel each one is important. They are now building a personal knowledge base of thoughts and feelings shared as the authors of their very own books. As your child crafts more stories for new books, the routine of authoring books will become second nature. At some point in this process, you will refer to his/her books as a personal collection and eventually "(Your Child's Name Here)'s Library".

9. Allow them to listen to their recorded stories anytime they want.

By allowing children to listen to their recorded selves, you are enabling them to get used to hearing themselves speak. This will be valuable in the future by securing speaking abilities, especially regarding open or public forums. After a while, you will also find them trying to follow along in their "books". This may be a lengthy process, but well worth the time involved.

10. Be patient with them, and they will soon be reading everything just as they read their stories!

Patience please, with new thoughts, there will be corrections. As children's abilities to process information become more efficient with realization of new knowledge with the occurrence of more precise characterization, you will notice the linking of processes and growth in your youngster's desire for bigger ideas and more elaborate displays of art. You both will feel those amazing accomplishments.

Teach your child that every symbol we use is simply a combination of circles, lines and dots. For example— 3 (two half circles); 5 (two lines and a half circle); M (four lines positioned to make what we call an M). Have them practice writing combinations of circles, lines and dots. They will soon learn how symbols need to be placed in order to make words.

Use index cards or paper and a pencil, marker or computer to make signs for everything in your living environment, (CHAIR, REFRIGERATOR, COUNTER, TOILET, BED...). Teach them that there is nothing complicated about reading and writing; they must simply learn the systems for those skills and practice them regularly. Also, teach them early that everything we do in our society is based on a system.

11. Connect words to pictures.

Most children are able to draw before they read and write. Give them a sheet of paper to draw about the stories they tell you. These can be included in their "books". As your child matures mentally the pictures will begin to match the words on the pages. Then you not only have an author, but an illustrator, as well.

12. Save your money for college.

Reading is the foundation of educational success. Setting this groundwork provides your child the gift of reading comprehension based on his own thoughts. Instilling this art of composition will prepare your child for unlimited future accomplishments.

Begin a savings account for your child's education. You have begun the process that will make the difference for the rest of your child's life!

Tried and True

I can remember Carrie's reading system, at 6 years of age, I spoke of how I love strawberries. I remember going into details about eating them. Carrie used a voice recorder to tape me, then she wrote out by hand what was recorded in my own words. I read it back and continued to add more. I believe that was my beginning to desire storytelling. I was basically illiterate at the time and having trouble in school, but her technique helped me to master my reading skills. I will be forever grateful to Carrie Peoples.

-Yaffa Lawson

I am excited to see this work in print. While visiting Carrie in 2012 just after the birth of my great grandson, Ty, she informed me of a program of hers that could have him reading before age 3. She printed the plan and gave it to me. As soon as Ty began to use words I put the program into action. By age 3 he amazed my family with the ability to read and recite the contents of THE BOOKS OF THE OLD TESTAMENT.

-Jean Ray